The Department of Homeland Security
The Department of Justice

Guidance to Assist Non-Federal Entities to Share Cyber Threat Indicators and Defensive Measures with Federal Entities under the Cybersecurity Information Sharing Act of 2015

June 15, 2016

Table of Contents

On December 18, 2015, Congress passed and President Obama signed into law the Cybersecurity Act of 2015. Title I of the Cybersecurity Act, entitled the Cybersecurity Information Sharing Act (CISA or the Act), provides increased authority for cybersecurity information sharing between and among the private sector; state, local, tribal, and territorial governments; and the Federal Government.[1] Section 105(a)(4) of the Act directed the Attorney General and the Secretary of the Department of Homeland Security (DHS) to jointly develop guidance to promote sharing of cyber threat indicators with federal entities pursuant to CISA no later than 60 days after CISA was enacted. That guidance was published on February 16, 2016, as required by statute.

Unlike other guidance documents that CISA required the federal government to produce, the guidance for sharing cyber threat indicators with federal entities did not direct the publication of an updated version. However, feedback elicited from non-federal entities after the release of the original guidance on sharing with federal entities counseled in favor of releasing a revised version, as permitted under section 105(a)(4)(B)(iii). Accordingly, this document clarifies and updates the original guidance to further assist non-federal entities who elect to share cyber threat indicators with the Federal Government to do so in accordance with the Act.[2] It also assists non-federal entities to identify defensive measures and explains how to share them with federal entities[3] as provided by CISA. Lastly, it describes the protections non-federal entities receive under CISA for sharing cyber threat indicators and defensive measures in accordance with the Act, including targeted liability protection and other statutory protections.[4]

1. Scope of Guidance

As required by Section 105(a)(4), this guidance addresses:

1. Identification of types of information that would qualify as a cyber threat indicator under the Act that would be unlikely to include information that is not directly related to a cybersecurity threat and is personal information of a specific individual or information that identifies a specific individual; and
2. Identification of types of information protected under otherwise applicable privacy laws that are unlikely to be directly related to a cybersecurity threat.[5]

---

[1] Section 104(c)(1) authorizes both the sharing and receipt of cyber threat indicators and defensive measures. In most cases, references throughout this document to the authority to share such information pursuant to section 104(c) also include the authority to receive the same information in accordance with section 104(c).

[2] This document does not provide guidance on reporting crimes to law enforcement. See section II for a discussion of sharing information for law enforcement, regulatory, and other purposes.

[3] Pursuant to CISA, "non-federal entity" means any private entity, non-Federal government agency or department, or state, tribal, or local government (including a political subdivision, department, or component thereof) and includes a government agency or department of the District of Columbia, the Commonwealth of Puerto Rico, the United States Virgin Islands, Guam, American Samoa, the Northern Mariana Islands, and any other territory or possession of the United States, but does not include a foreign power as defined in section 101 of the Foreign Intelligence Surveillance Act of 1978 (50 U.S.C. § 1801). Section 102(14)(A)-(C).

[4] This document focuses on providing guidance to non-federal entities concerning how they may properly share cyber threat indicators with the government pursuant to CISA. For policies and procedures specifically addressing the protection of individual rights for activities conducted under the Act, please refer to the jointly published Privacy and Civil Liberties Interim Guidance at https://www.us-cert.gov/ais.

[5] This guidance is intended as assistance, not authority. It has no regulatory effect, confers no rights or remedies, and does not have the force of law. *See United States v. Caceres*, 440 U.S. 741 (1979). Further, the sharing of a

It also explains how to identify and share defensive measures, even though section 105(a)(4) does not require the guidance to do so.[6]

In addition to covering how to identify and share cyber threat indicators and defensive measures, this guidance also explains how to share that information with federal entities through the Federal Government's capability and process that is operated by DHS (See section 3.B.) Furthermore, it explains how to share such information with DHS and other federal entities—including law enforcement—through other means authorized by the Act, and discusses the various legal protections the Act provides for such authorized sharing (See sections 3.C. and 4).

2. Key Concepts

The Act authorizes sharing of specific information that is used to protect information systems and information. Section 104(c) allows non-federal entities to share cyber threat indicators and defensive measures with any other entity—private, federal, state, local, territorial, or tribal—for a "cybersecurity purpose." The Act defines a "cybersecurity purpose" as the purpose of protecting an information system or information that is stored on, processed by, or transiting an information system from a cybersecurity threat or security vulnerability. Section 102(4). The terms "cyber threat indicator" and "defensive measure" also have specific meanings under the Act. These key concepts and associated terms are discussed below.

a. Cyber Threat Indicator

The Act defines a cyber threat indicator to mean information that is necessary to describe or identify:

- Malicious reconnaissance, including anomalous patterns of communications that appear to be transmitted for the purpose of gathering technical information related to a cybersecurity threat or security vulnerability; [7]

---

cyber threat indicator or defensive measure with a non-federal entity under the Act shall not create a right or benefit to similar information by such non-federal entity or any other non-federal entity. Section 104(f).

[6] Although section 105(a)(4) omits any reference to defensive measures, we have elected to include them in this guidance because the Act authorizes non-federal entities to share defensive measures. Section 104(c). Furthermore, providing guidance to non-federal entities on sharing defensive measures is important because improperly shared information is not eligible for the Act's protections.

[7] The definition of cyber threat indicator references a "cybersecurity threat" and "security vulnerability," which are terms defined by the Act. A cybersecurity threat is defined under section 102(5) to mean:

> An action, not protected by the First Amendment to the Constitution of the United States, on or through an information system that may result in an unauthorized effort to adversely impact the security, availability, confidentiality, or integrity of an information system or information that is stored on, processed by, or transiting an information system. The term "cybersecurity threat" does not include any action that solely involves a violation of a consumer term of service or a consumer licensing agreement.

Many terms of service agreements prohibit activities that satisfy the definition of a "cybersecurity threat." However, activities that are "solely" violations of consumer agreements but do not otherwise meet the definition are not cybersecurity threats under CISA.

- A method of defeating a security control or exploitation of a security vulnerability;
- A security vulnerability, including anomalous activity that appears to indicate the existence of a security vulnerability;
- A method of causing a user with legitimate access to an information system or information that is stored on, processed by, or transiting an information system to unwittingly enable the defeat of a security control or exploitation of a security vulnerability;
- Malicious cyber command and control;
- The actual or potential harm caused by an incident, including a description of the information exfiltrated as a result of a particular cybersecurity threat;
- Any other attribute of a cybersecurity threat, if disclosure of such attribute is not otherwise prohibited by law; or
- Any combination thereof.[8]

The Act promotes the goal of sharing while simultaneously providing privacy protections in two ways: first, by specifying the types of cyber threat information that can be shared under the Act between and among non-federal and federal entities; and, second, by limiting sharing under the Act only to those circumstances in which such information is necessary to describe or identify threats to information and information systems. Effectively, the only information that can be shared under the Act is information that is directly related to and necessary to identify or describe a cybersecurity threat.

Information is not directly related to a cybersecurity threat if it is not necessary to detect, prevent, or mitigate the cybersecurity threat. For example, a cyber threat indicator could be centered on a spear phishing email. For a phishing email, personal information about the sender of email ("From"/"Sender" address), a malicious URL in the e-mail, malware files attached to the e-mail, the content of the e-mail, and additional email information related to the malicious email or potential cybersecurity threat actor, such as Subject Line, Message ID, and X-Mailer, could be considered directly related to a cybersecurity threat. The name and e-mail address of the targets of the email (i.e., the "To" address), however, would be personal information not directly related to a cybersecurity threat and therefore should not typically be included as part of the cyber threat indicator.

The following are additional examples of information that would contain cyber threat indicators that a private entity could submit to DHS and other federal entities under CISA:

The definition of a cybersecurity threat includes activities that may have unauthorized and negative results, but excludes authorized activities, such as extensive use of bandwidth that may incidentally cause adverse effects. S. Rep. No. 114-32 at 4. This definition clearly allows the sharing of information related to criminal hacking actions like theft of information or destruction of property.

A security vulnerability is defined by section 102(17) to mean "any attribute of hardware, software, process, or procedure that could enable or facilitate the defeat of a security control." In contrast to a cybersecurity threat, it does not require adverse impact to an information system or information.

[8] Section 102(6).

- A company could report that its web server log files show that a particular IP address has sent web traffic that appears to be testing whether the company's content management system has not been updated to patch a recent vulnerability.
- A security researcher could report on her discovery of a technique that permits unauthorized access to an industrial control system.
- A software publisher could report a vulnerability it has discovered in its software.
- A managed security service company could report a pattern of domain name lookups that it believes correspond to malware infection.
- A manufacturer could report unexecuted malware found on its network.
- A researcher could report on the domain names or IP addresses associated with botnet command and control servers.
- An engineering company that suffers a computer intrusion could describe the types of engineering files that appear to have been exfiltrated, as a way of warning other companies with similar assets.
- A newspaper suffering a distributed denial of service attack to its web site could report the IP addresses that are sending malicious traffic.

To help ensure consistency with CISA's definitions and requirements, standardized fields in structured formats can be used to establish a profile that limits the type of information in a cyber threat indicator. Much of the information within an indicator is centered on an observable fact about the cyber threat. For example, a cyber threat indicator has a variety of observable characteristics: a malicious email, internet protocol (IP) addresses, file hashes, domain names, uniform resource locators (URLs), malware files, and malware artifacts (attributes about a file). The specificity and nature of the observable facts are designed to reduce the risk that a cyber threat indicator contains personal content or information inappropriate to share. DHS's Automated Indicator Sharing (AIS) initiative uses this means of controlling the type of information that may be shared using the automated system discussed in section 3.B.i.

b. Defensive Measure

The Act defines a defensive measure to mean:

> An action, device, procedure, signature, technique, or other measure applied to an information system or information that is stored on, processed by, or transiting an information system that detects, prevents, or mitigates a known or suspected cybersecurity threat or security vulnerability. The term "defensive measure" does not include a measure that destroys, renders unusable, provides unauthorized access to, or substantially harms an information system or information stored on, processed by, or transiting such information system not owned by the private entity operating the measure; or another entity or Federal entity that is authorized to provide consent and has provided consent to that private entity for operation of such measure.

For example, a defensive measure could be something as simple as a security device that protects or limits access to a company's computer infrastructure or as complex as using sophisticated software tools to detect and protect against anomalous and unauthorized activities on a company's information system.

Similar to a cyber threat indicator, a defensive measure under the Act typically will not include personal information of a specific individual or information that identifies a specific individual. Instead, it will generally consist principally of technical information that can be used to detect and counter a cybersecurity threat.[9] However, personal information of a specific individual or information that identifies a specific individual may occasionally be necessary to describe a cybersecurity threat, as is also true of a cyber threat indicator. For example, a signature or technique for protecting against targeted exploits such as spear phishing may include a specific email address from which malicious emails are being sent.

Some examples of defensive measures include but are not limited to:

- A computer program that identifies a pattern of malicious activity in web traffic flowing into an organization.
- A signature that could be loaded into a company's intrusion detection system in order to detect a spear phishing campaign with particular characteristics.
- A firewall rule that disallows a type of malicious traffic from entering a network.
- An algorithm that can search through a cache of network traffic to discover anomalous patterns that may indicate malicious activity.
- A technique for quickly matching, in an automated manner, the content of an organization's incoming Simple Mail Transfer Protocol (SMTP, a protocol commonly used for email) traffic against a set of content known to be associated with a specific cybersecurity threat without unacceptably degrading the speed of email delivery to end users.

c. Information Protected under Otherwise Applicable Privacy Laws that are Unlikely to Be Directly Related to a Cybersecurity Threat

Under section 104(c), a non-federal entity may share a cyber threat indicator or defensive measure for a cybersecurity purpose "notwithstanding any other provision of law." Consequently, otherwise conflicting laws, including privacy laws, do not restrict sharing or any other action undertaken pursuant to CISA. But to safeguard privacy while also promoting

---

[9] When developing and implementing defensive measures pursuant to section 104(b), due diligence should be exercised to ensure that they do not unlawfully access or damage information systems or data. CISA's definition of and authorization to use a defensive measure (sections 102(7) and 104(b), respectively) do not permit unauthorized access to or execution of computer code on another entity's information systems or other actions that would substantially harm another entity's information systems. Joint Explanatory Statement to Accompany the Cybersecurity Act of 2015, p. 2, available at
http://intelligence.house.gov/sites/intelligence.house.gov/files/documents/JES%20for%20Cybersecurity%20Act%20of%202015.pdf. Cognizant of the fact that defensive measures deployed on one entity's network could have effects on other networks, Congress defined a defensive measure to only include measures on an entity's information systems that do not cause substantial harm to another entity's information systems or data. Even if a defensive measure does not cause such substantial harm, it is still not within CISA's definition if it enables unauthorized access to another entity's information systems.

information sharing, CISA requires a non-federal entity to remove any information from a cyber threat indicator or defensive measure that it knows at the time of sharing to be personal information of a specific individual or information that identifies a specific individual that is not directly related to a cybersecurity threat before sharing that cyber threat indicator or defensive measure with a federal entity. Section 104(d)(2).

Non-Federal Entity Sharing Under CISA

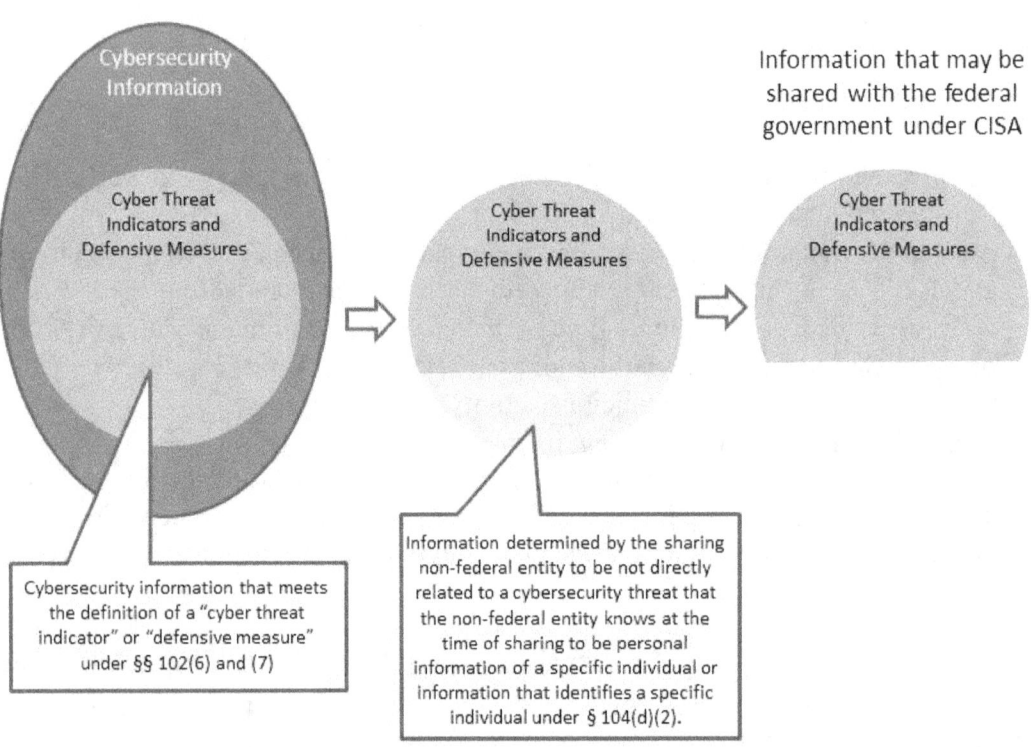

Yet, some of the categories of information below may be used in connection with a cybersecurity threat, such as social engineering attacks, and may, therefore, be shareable as part of a cyber threat indicator or defensive measure. Even so, sharing them in a form that constitutes or includes personal information of a specific individual or information that identifies a specific individual may not be necessary. For instance, while sharing the medical condition of a particular individual targeted for a phishing attack is unlikely to be useful or directly related to a cybersecurity threat, sharing an anonymized characterization of the cyber threat may have utility.

To assist in the task of identifying shareable information, section 105(a)(4)(B)(ii) requires this guidance to help entities identify certain types of information protected under otherwise applicable privacy laws that are unlikely to be directly related to a cybersecurity threat. As explained above, cyber threat indicators and defensive measures will typically consist of technical information that describes attributes of a cybersecurity threat that generally need not include various categories of information that are considered sensitive and, therefore, protected by privacy laws. Information unlikely to be directly related to a cybersecurity threat falling into this category of information protected under otherwise applicable privacy law may include:[10]

- Protected Health Information (PHI), which is defined as individually identifiable health information transmitted or maintained by a covered entity or its business associates in any form or medium (45 CFR 160.103). PHI is information, including demographic information, that relates to:

  o the individual's past, present, or future physical or mental health or condition,
  o the provision of health care to the individual, or
  o the past, present, or future payment for the provision of health care to the individual, and that identifies the individual or for which there is a reasonable basis to believe can be used to identify the individual. Protected health information includes many common identifiers (e.g., name, address, birth date, Social Security Number) when they can be associated with the health information listed above.

  For example, a medical record, laboratory report, or hospital bill would be PHI because each document would contain a patient's name and/or other identifying information associated with the health data content.

- Human Resource Information is information contained within an employee's personnel file, such as hiring decisions, performance reviews, and disciplinary actions.

- Consumer Information/History may include information related to an individual's purchases, preferences, complaints and even credit. The Fair Credit Reporting Act (FCRA) requires that consumer reporting agencies adopt reasonable procedures for meeting the needs of commerce for consumer credit, personnel, insurance, and other information in a manner which is fair and equitable to the consumer, with regard to the confidentiality, accuracy, relevancy, and proper utilization of such information.

- Education History relates to an individual's education, such as transcripts, or training, such as professional certifications. The Family Educational Rights and Privacy Act (FERPA) (20 U.S.C. § 1232g; 34 CFR Part 99) is a federal law that protects the privacy of student education records. The law applies to all schools that receive funds under an applicable program of the U.S. Department of Education.

- Financial Information constitutes a vast category of information that is highly sensitive and highly regulated. Financial information includes anything from bank statements, to loan information, to credit reports. Certain laws, such as the Gramm-Leach-Bliley Act require financial institutions – companies that offer consumers financial products or services like loans, financial or investment advice, or insurance – to explain their information-sharing practices to their customers and to safeguard sensitive data.

---

[10] The discussion of potentially relevant privacy laws mentioned below is not intended to be exhaustive.

- Identifying information about property ownership may be protected by privacy laws. Although some information about property ownership may be publicly available, such as property purchase records, other information such as Vehicle Identification Numbers are inherently more sensitive and typically governed by state laws.

- Identifying information of children under the age of 13 is subject to certain requirements under the Children's Online Privacy Protection Act (COPPA), which imposed certain requirements on operators of websites or online services directed to children under 13 years of age, and on operators of other websites or online services that have actual knowledge that they are collecting personal information online from a child under 13 years of age.

In particular, the content of communications may be more likely to contain sensitive or protected information such as those found in the categories listed above. Thus, non-federal entities should exercise particular care when reviewing such information before sharing it with a federal entity.

3. How to Share Cyber Threat Indicators and Defensive Measures with the Federal Government

The Act authorizes non-federal entities to share cyber threat indicators and defensive measures with federal entities—and non-federal entities—as provided by section 104(c). Section 105(c) specifically provides for sharing such information through the Federal Government's capability and process for receiving cyber threat indicators and defensive measures, which is operated by DHS pursuant to section 105(c). That capability and process was certified as operational by the Secretary of DHS on March 17, 2016, as required by CISA.

The manner in which information is shared affects the protections private entities receive for sharing cyber threat indicators and defensive measures. Section 104(c) authorizes sharing of cyber threat indicators and defensive measures for a cybersecurity purpose and notwithstanding any other provision of law. As discussed further below, such sharing receives liability protection under section 106(b)(2) when conducted with the federal government through the DHS capability and process, or as otherwise permitted under section 105(c)(1)(B).[11] In addition to sharing conducted as provided for under section 105(c)(1)(B), section 104(c) also authorizes other sharing of cyber threat indicators and defensive measures with any federal entity, including sector-specific agencies; however, sharing that is not consistent with section 105(c)(1)(B) will not receive liability protection under the Act, even if a federal entity receiving the information shares it with DHS immediately upon receipt. Even though sharing conducted pursuant to section 104(c) but not consistent with section 105(c)(1)(B) does not receive liability protection (e.g., sharing with a federal entity that is not conducted through the DHS capability and process in section 105(c)), it still receives a variety of other protections that cover all sharing conducted

---

[11] While not the focus of this guidance, private entities also receive liability protection under section 106(b)(1) for sharing cyber threat indicators and defensive measures with other private entities in accordance with CISA. See Chart in Appendix 1.

pursuant section 104(c). Those protections are further discussed in section 5. (See also Chart on page 19-20)

CISA only authorizes information sharing for a cybersecurity purpose.[12] It does not limit or modify any existing information sharing or reporting relationship, prohibit an existing or require a new information sharing relationship, or mandate the use of the capability and process within DHS developed under section 105(c). Section 108(f). Sharing that is not conducted in accordance with the Act is not eligible for any of the Act's protections. Sharing or reporting may be eligible for other protections if appropriately conducted under the auspices of other laws or regulations.

Sharing conducted through the means discussed in this guidance pursuant to CISA should not be construed to satisfy any statutory, regulatory, or contractual obligation. It is not a substitute for voluntary or required reporting of information to federal entities, such as known or suspected cybercrimes directly to appropriate law enforcement agencies, known or suspected cyber incidents directly to the National Cybersecurity and Communications Integration Center, or required reporting to regulatory entities. The sharing addressed in this guidance is intended to complement, not replace, the prompt reporting of any criminal activity, cyber incidents, or reportable events to the appropriate authorities.

a. Requirements for Non-Federal Entities Sharing Cyber Threat Indicators and Defensive Measures with Federal Entities

CISA's information sharing authorization and liability and other protections for information sharing only attach to sharing cyber threat indicators and defensive measures, as those terms are defined by the Act. CISA does not cover the sharing of information that falls outside the definition of those terms. For example, the entire contents of a hard drive of a personal computer that has been compromised by a cyber threat actor would be unlikely to solely contain information constituting a cyber threat indicator or defensive measure, thus sharing it in its entirety may fall outside the scope of CISA. However, sharing cyber threat indicators extracted from the hard drive of a compromised computer would be eligible for CISA's protections if done in accordance with CISA's requirements. The same reasoning applies to sharing network logs or other similar artifacts gathered during an incident response.

Furthermore, under section 104(d)(2)(A), a non-federal entity must review cyber threat indicators prior to sharing them to assess whether they contain any information not directly related to a cybersecurity threat that the non-federal entity knows at the time of sharing to be personal information of a specific individual or information that identifies a specific individual and remove such information. While not explicitly required by the Act, non-federal entities are encouraged to conduct a similar review prior to sharing defensive measures under the Act. A defensive measure may contain a cyber threat indicator. Consequently, even though CISA may not require the removal of personal information for a defensive measure under section

---

[12] CISA also does not prohibit or permit the sharing of information for any reason other than a cybersecurity purpose. Sharing for any other purpose is governed by other legal authorities.

104(d)(2)(A), removal may nevertheless be required for information within the defensive measure that is also a cyber threat indicator.

If a non-federal entity does not "know at the time of sharing" that a cyber threat indicator contains personal information of a specific individual or information that identifies a specific individual, the non-federal entity is not required to alter the shared information. A non-federal entity may conduct its review for such information using either a manual or technical process; either is permissible under CISA. Section 104(d)(2)(A) and (B).[13]

b. Non-Federal Entities Sharing Cyber Threat Indicators and Defensive Measures through the Real-Time DHS Capability and Process

Section 105(c) of the Act directs the Secretary of DHS to develop a capability and process within DHS that will accept cyber threat indicators and defensive measures in real time from any non-federal entity, including private entities. Non-federal entities may share such information with DHS through this capability and process, and DHS will in turn relay that information to federal entities in an automated manner,[14] as required by the Act and consistent with the operational and privacy and civil liberties policies instituted under sections 105(a) and (b).[15] Upon certification by the Secretary of Homeland Security in accordance with section 105(c), the DHS capability and process became the process by which the Federal Government receives cyber threat indicators and defensive measures under the Act that are shared by a non-federal entity with the Federal Government through electronic mail or media, an interactive form on an Internet website, or a real time, automated process between information systems, with the specific exception of the other means of sharing discussed below in section (c) of this document.

Provided that sharing is otherwise conducted in accordance with the Act, sharing conducted using this DHS capability will receive liability protection under section 106(b). It will also receive the other protections provided by the Act discussed more fully below in section 5. The implementation of this capability does not, however, limit or prohibit otherwise lawful disclosures of communications, records, or other information, including the reporting of known or suspected criminal activity. Section 105(c)(1)(e). It also does not limit or prohibit voluntary or legally compelled participation in a federal law enforcement investigation or affect the provision of cyber threat indicators or defensive measures as part of a contractual requirement. Section 105(a)(1)(E).

---

[13]   Although not directly relevant to this guidance on information sharing between non-federal and federal entities, non-federal entities should remain mindful that CISA requires non-federal entities to implement and utilize a security control to protect against unauthorized access to or acquisition of shared cyber threat indicator or defensive measure. Section 104(d)(1).

[14]   Section 105(a)(3)(A) requires DHS to disseminate cyber threat indicators and defensive measures shared with DHS pursuant to section 105(c) to the Departments of Commerce, Defense, Energy, Homeland Security, Justice, Treasury, and the Office of the Director of National Intelligence in an automated fashion. Section 105(a)(3)(A)(i).

[15] The Privacy and Civil Liberties Guidelines and Operational Procedures are available at https://www.us-cert.gov/ais.

Non-federal entities may share cyber threat indicators and defensive measures through the DHS capability and process created under section 105(c) via the AIS initiative, web form, email, or other information sharing programs that use these means of receiving cyber threat indicators or defensive measures. Sharing conducted using any of these means is eligible for liability protection, as well as CISA's other protections and exemptions. Instructions on utilizing each method can be found below.

i.   Automated Indicator Sharing (AIS)

Non-federal entities may share cyber threat indicators and defensive measures with federal entities using DHS's AIS initiative, which enables the timely exchange of cyber threat indicators and defensive measures among the private sector, state, local, tribal, and territorial governments and the Federal government. AIS leverages a technical specification for the format and exchange of cyber threat indicators and defensive measures using the Structured Threat Information eXchange (STIX) and Trusted Automated eXchange of Indicator Information (TAXII), respectively. By using standardized fields (STIX) and communication (TAXII), DHS enables organizations to share structured cyber threat information in a secure and automated manner.

In order to share cyber threat indicators and defensive measures through AIS, participants acquire their own TAXII client that will communicate with the DHS TAXII server. AIS participants also execute the AIS Terms of Use, and follow submission guidance that outlines the type of information that should and should not be provided when submitting cyber threat indicators and defensive measures through AIS.

Once a cyber threat indicator or defensive measure is received, analyzed, and sanitized, AIS will share the indicator or defensive measure with all AIS participants. AIS will not provide the identity of the submitting entity to other AIS participants unless the submitter consents to share its identity as the source of the cyber threat indicator submission.

Cyber threat indicators and defensive measures submitted via automated means including AIS are considered part of the DHS capability and process created under section 105(c) and, therefore, eligible for liability protection, as well as CISA's other protections and exemptions. For more information on AIS, visit the AIS web page at https://www.us-cert.gov/ais. Entities wishing to connect to AIS may send an email to the address listed at https://www.us-cert.gov/ais.

ii.   Web Form

Non-federal entities may share cyber threat indicators and defensive measures with DHS's National Cybersecurity and Communications Integration Center by filling out a web form on a DHS website (including us-cert.gov). Cyber threat indicators and defensive measures submitted via web form to the National Cybersecurity and Communications Integration Center are considered part of the DHS capability and process created under section 105(c) and, therefore, eligible for liability protection, as well as CISA's other protections and exemptions. For more information, non-federal entities may visit the web page at https://www.us-cert.gov/ais.

iii. Email

Non-federal entities may share cyber threat indicators and defensive measures with DHS's National Cybersecurity and Communications Integration Center by sending an email to DHS. Cyber threat indicators and defensive measures submitted via email are considered part of the DHS capability and process created under section 105(c) and, therefore, eligible for liability protection, as well as CISA's other protections and exemptions. For more information, non-federal entities may visit the web page at https://www.us-cert.gov/ais.

iv. Other DHS Programs through which Cyber Threat Indicators and Defensive Measures May Be Shared Using the DHS Capability and Process

Non-federal entities may also share cyber threat indicators and defensive measures with DHS's National Cybersecurity and Communications Integration Center by sharing within programs that leverage automated machine-to-machine sharing, web forms or email. For example, DHS provides access to communities of interest (such as industrial control systems owners and operators) through a web-based portal, which allows sharing of indicators via web form or secure messaging capabilities within the portal. Stakeholders participating in DHS's Cybersecurity Information Sharing and Collaboration Program may share cyber threat indicators or defensive measures within that program, leveraging automated machine-to-machine sharing, web forms or email. Any sharing of cyber threat indicators or defensive measures with DHS's National Cybersecurity and Communications Integration Center using one of these methods for sharing is considered to be sharing with DHS's capability and process created under section 105(c) and, therefore, eligible for liability protection, as well as CISA's other protections and exemptions.

v. Information Sharing and Analysis Organizations and Centers

Under section 104(c), non-federal entities may also share cyber threat indicators and defensive measures with federal entities through Information Sharing and Analysis Centers (ISACs) or Information Sharing and Analysis Organizations (ISAOs), which may share them with federal entities through DHS on their behalf. In general, ISACs and ISAOs are private entities. Under section 106(b)(1), private entities that share a cyber threat indicator or defensive measure with an ISAC or ISAO in accordance with the Act receive liability protection and other protections and exemptions for such sharing.[16] Similarly, ISACs and ISAOs that share information with other private entities in accordance with the Act also receive liability protection under section 106(b)(1), as well as other protections and exemptions. Likewise, an ISAC or ISAO that shares cyber threat indicators or defensive measures with the federal government in accordance with section 104(c) through the DHS capability and process created under section 105(c), or as otherwise consistent with section 105(c)(1)(B), is also eligible for liability protection under section 106(b)(2), in addition to CISA's other protections and exemptions.

---

[16] The topic of sharing between non-governmental entities is further addressed at Annex 1.

c. Non-Federal Entities Sharing with Federal Entities through Means Other than the DHS Capability and Process

Consistent with CISA, non-federal entities may also share cyber threat indicators and defensive measures with federal entities through means other than the Federal government's capability and process operated by DHS described in sections b.(i) through (v) above. Section 104(c) authorizes, notwithstanding any provision of law, a non-federal entity to share cyber threat indicators and defensive measures with a federal entity—or any non-federal entity—so long as sharing is conducted for a cybersecurity purpose. Section 106(b)'s protection from liability, however, only covers such sharing where a private entity shares cyber threat indicators or defensive measures with the federal government "consistent with" section 105(c)(1)(B). Sections b.(i) through (iv) above discuss the DHS capability and process provided for in section 105(c)(1)(B). Sections 105(c)(1)(B)(i) and (ii) of CISA describe two additional means of liability-protected sharing.

First, section 105(c)(1)(B)(i) allows the sharing of "communications," consistent with section 104, between a federal and non-federal entity regarding previously shared cyber threat indicator to describe the relevant cybersecurity threat or to develop a defensive measure based on such cyber threat indicator. This section would apply when a non-federal entity first shares a cyber threat indicator with the DHS capability and process or a regulator as permitted by section 105(c)(1)(B)(ii) discussed below, and then engages in communications with a federal entity regarding that previously shared indicator. Section 104 only permits sharing of cyber threat indicators and defensive measures for cybersecurity purposes (section 104(c)) and requires removal of certain irrelevant personal information prior to such sharing (section 104(d)(2)).

Second, section 105(c)(1)(B)(ii) also permits communications between a regulated non-federal entity and its Federal regulatory authority regarding a cybersecurity threat. Unlike section 105(c)(1)(B)(i), it is not expressly limited to communications about a previously shared communication.

While both sections 105(c)(1)(B)(i) and (ii) discuss the sharing of "communications," only the sharing of cyber threat indicators and defensive measures receive liability protection under section 106(b). Moreover, sharing under section 106(b)(1) must otherwise be conducted in accordance with CISA to receive liability protection. Accordingly, liability protection for sharing under both sections 105(c)(1)(B)(i) and (ii) requires adherence to all of CISA's requirements (e.g., removal of certain personal information pursuant to section 104(d)(2), sharing cyber threat indicators or a defensive measure and sharing for a cybersecurity purpose).

4. Other Protections Received by Sharing Entities

In addition to the liability protections discussed above, the Act provides other protection to sharing entities and protects information shared in accordance with the Act. Sharing with the federal government *other than* in a manner consistent with section 105(c)(1)(B) does not receive liability protection under the Act; however, such sharing is eligible for all of the other protections furnished by the Act, just the same as sharing conducted with DHS under section 105(c).

Other than liability protection, CISA provides the following protections for sharing cyber threat indicators and defensive measures with any federal entity conducted pursuant to section 104(c):

- Antitrust Exemption: The Act provides a statutory exemption to federal antitrust laws for the sharing between and among private entities of cyber threat indicators, defensive measures, or assistance relating to the prevention, investigation, or mitigation of a cybersecurity threat for a cybersecurity purpose. Section 104(e). It supplements the policy statement issued by the Department of Justice's Antitrust Division and the Federal Trade Commission in May 2014 stating that sharing of cyber threat information would in the normal course be unlikely to violate federal antitrust laws.[17] The Act also expressly prohibits conduct that would otherwise constitute an antitrust violation, notwithstanding the exception provided by section 104(e)(1) to prevent this exception from being used as the basis for committing antitrust violations under the guise of cybersecurity information sharing. Section 108(e).

- Exemption from federal and state disclosure laws: The Act provides that cyber threat indicators or defensive measures shared with the federal government under CISA are exempt from disclosure under federal state, tribal, or local government freedom of information law, open government law, open meetings law, open records law, sunshine law, or similar law requiring disclosure of information or records. Section 104(d)(4)(B); section 105(d)(3). Shared information is also deemed "voluntarily shared," which assists in protecting appropriately shared information from disclosure under The Critical Infrastructure Information Act of 2002.

- Exemption from certain state and federal regulatory uses: Cyber threat indicators and defensive measures shared with the federal government under the Act shall not be used by any federal, state, tribal, or local government to regulate, including through an enforcement action, the lawful activity of any non-federal entity or any activity taken by a non-federal entity pursuant to mandatory standards, including an activity relating to monitoring, operating a defensive measure, or sharing of a cyber threat indicator. However, a cyber threat indicator or defensive measure may, consistent with a federal, state, tribal, or local government regulatory authority specifically relating to the prevention or mitigation of cybersecurity threats to information systems, inform the development or implementation of a regulation relating to such information systems. CISA's legislative history states that congressional drafters viewed this as a narrow exception to ensure that government agencies with regulatory authority understand the current landscape of cyber threats and those facing the particular regulatory sector over which they have cognizance. Section 104(d)(4)(C); section 105(d)(5)(D).

---

[17] The DOJ/FTC policy statement revisited a business review letter prepared by the Antitrust Division in 2000 in which it examined a proposed cybersecurity information sharing program. The policy statement reaffirmed the conclusions of the 2000 business review letter. It stated, "While this guidance is now over a decade old, it remains the Agencies' current analysis that properly designed sharing of cybersecurity threat information is not likely to raise antitrust concerns." Policy Statement at 1, *available at* http://www.justice.gov/sites/default/files/atr/legacy/2014/04/10/305027.pdf .

- <u>No waiver of privilege for shared material</u>: Under the Act, sharing cyber threat indicators and defensive measures with the federal government does not constitute the waiver of any applicable privilege or protection provided by law; in particular, shared information does not surrender trade secret protection. Section 105(d)(1).

- <u>Treatment of commercial, financial, and proprietary information</u>: When so designated by the sharing entity, shared information shall be treated as commercial, financial, and proprietary information. The legislative history indicates that Congress expected the Federal government to further share and use such information for cybersecurity purposes consistent with the privileges, protections, and any claims of propriety on such information. Section 105(d)(2).

- <u>Ex parte communications waiver</u>: Under the Act, the sharing of cyber threat indicators and defensive measures with the federal government under the Act shall not be subject to the rules of any Federal agency or department or any judicial doctrine regarding ex parte communications with a decision-making official. This provision addresses concerns about ex parte communications related to the Administrative Procedure Act (APA), 5 U.S.C. § 553. Section 105(d)(4).

The applicability of the protections above varies depending on the nature of the entity sharing information with the Federal Government. All of CISA's protections, including liability protection, are available to private entities, which CISA defines to include private companies and other private organizations, as well as "State, tribal, or local government performing utility services, such as electric, natural gas, or water services." Section 102(15)(B). In addition to private entities, CISA's definition of "non-federal entities" includes other State, tribal, or local government entities. But such non-federal entities are not eligible for liability protection or antitrust protection, which is reserved for "private entities." Sections 106(b), 104(e). They are, however, eligible for CISA's other protections discussed above. Sharing cyber threat indicators and defensive measures with State, tribal, or local government entities is exempt from state disclosure laws. Section 104(d)(4)(B). Furthermore, CISA limits regulatory use of such shared information by a State, tribal, or local government. Section 104(d)(4)(C).

Protection for Sharing with Federal Entities under CISA

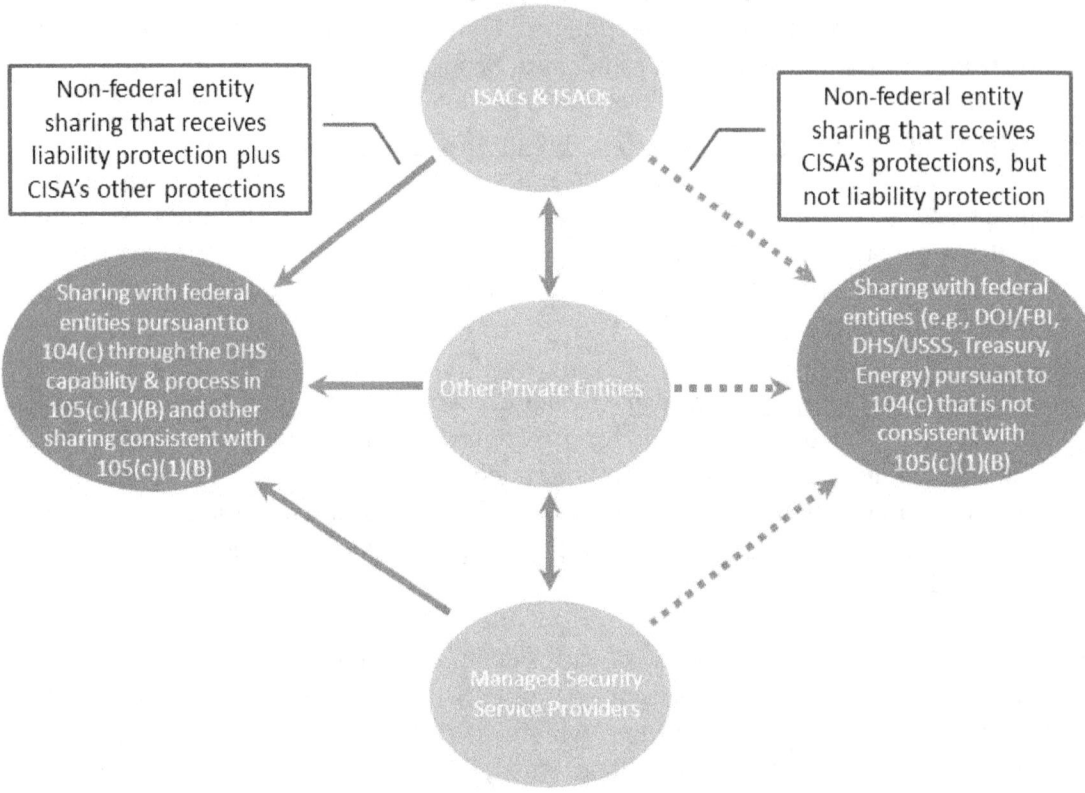

Sharing Cyber Threat Indicators and Defensive Measures with a Federal Entity					
Means of Sharing	Authority for Sharing	Liability Protection Provision	Receiving Federal Entity	Requirements	Protections Conferred for Sharing Under the Act
DHS Capability and Associated Programs and other sharing permitted under section 105(c)(1)(B)	Sections 104(c) and 105(c)(1)(B)	Section 106(b)(2)	DHS	• Sharing for a cybersecurity purpose. Section 104(c) • Sharing cyber threat indicators & defensive measures. Sections 104(c) and 106(b)(2) • Implement and utilize a security control to protect against unauthorized access to or acquisition of cyber threat indicators or defensive measures. Section 104(d)(1) • Removal prior to sharing using a manual or technical means of information not directly related to a cybersecurity threat that the private entity knows at the time of sharing to be personal information of a specific person or information identifying a specific person. Section 104(d)(2)(A) and (B) • When receiving cyber threat indicators from the government observe lawful restrictions placed by a private entity. Section 104(c)(2) • Compliance with procedures for submission to DHS	• Liability protection for sharing of cyber threat indicators. Section 106(b) • Exemption from state disclosure laws. Section 104(d)(4)(B) * • Exemption from state regulatory use. Section 104(d)(4)(C) * • No waiver of privilege for shared material. Section 105(d)(1) • Treatment of commercial, financial, and proprietary information. Section 105(d)(2) • Exemption from federal disclosure laws. Section 105(d)(3) • Ex parte communications waiver. Section 105(d)(4) • Exemption from federal regulatory use. Section 105(d)(5)(D)

* This exemption applies to indicators and defensive measures shared with a State, tribal, or local government entity rather than with a federal entity; however, it is included here in the interest of completeness.

Sharing Cyber Threat Indicators and Defensive Measures with a Federal Entity (Continued)					
Means of Sharing	Authority for Sharing	Liability Protection Provision	Receiving Federal Entity	Requirements	Protections Conferred for Sharing Under the Act
Any other sharing conducted under the Act	Section 104(c)	N/A	Any federal entity (e.g., FBI, DHS, DOE, Treasury, DoD)	• Sharing for a cybersecurity purpose. Section 104(c) • Sharing cyber threat indicators & defensive measures. Sections 104(c) and 106(b)(2) • Implement and utilize a security control to protect against unauthorized access to or acquisition of cyber threat indicators or defensive measures. Section 104(d)(1) • Removal prior to sharing using a manual or technical means of information not directly related to a cybersecurity threat that the private entity knows at the time of sharing to be personal information of a specific person or information identifying a specific person. Section 104(d)(2)(A) and (B) • When receiving cyber threat indicators from the government observe lawful restrictions placed by a private entity. Section 104(c)(2)	• Exemption from state disclosure laws. Section 104(d)(4)(B) * • Exemption from state regulatory use. Section 104(d)(4)(C) * • No waiver of privilege for shared material. Section 105(d)(1) • Treatment of commercial, financial, and proprietary information. Section 105(d)(2) • Exemption from federal disclosure laws. Section 105(d)(3) • Ex parte communications waiver. Section 105(d)(4) • Exemption from federal regulatory use. Section 105(d)(5)(D)

* This exemption applies to indicators and defensive measures shared with a State, tribal, or local government entity rather than with a federal entity; however, it is included here in the interest of completeness.

5. **Annex 1: Sharing of Cyber Threat Indicator and Defensive Measure Sharing between Non-Governmental Entities under CISA**

Section 105(a)(4) does not direct the federal government to produce guidance covering how private entities may share cyber threat indicators and defensive measures with each other under CISA. However, multiple private organizations have requested such guidance to facilitate their information sharing practices. Accordingly, the following chart furnishes a summary of the protections and exemptions that non-governmental entities receive for sharing cyber threat indicators and defensive measures with each other in accordance with CISA.

CISA authorizes private entities to share cyber threat indicators and defensive measures with other private entities (section 104(c)). It also provides private entities with liability protection for conducting such sharing in accordance with CISA. Section 106(b)(1). In general, private entities include ISACs, ISAOs, and cybersecurity and managed security services providers. It is noteworthy that CISA's definition of a private entity includes a State, tribal, or local government that performs utility services. Section 102(15)(B). The chart below addresses only protections available for sharing between non-governmental entities, and so uses the term "non-governmental entity" in lieu of "private entity."

Sharing between private entities, regardless of whether they are non-governmental, is subject to the same requirements as sharing between private and non-federal entities discussed above. For instance, under CISA only cyber threat indicators and defensive measures may be shared, and the removal of certain personal information pursuant to section 104(d)(2) is required. Some of the protections discussed above do not apply to information sharing between non-governmental entities because those protections only cover information shared with governmental entities (e.g., federal and state disclosure laws). In the event a non-governmental entity shares a cyber threat indicator or defensive measure with another non-governmental entity, and the receiving non-governmental entity subsequently shares that information with a federal or state entity, those additional protections would then apply to the information that was shared with a federal entity, as discussed above.

Sharing Cyber Threat Indicators and Defensive Measures between Non-Governmental Entities			
Authority for Sharing & Receiving	Liability Protection Provision	Requirements	Protections Conferred for Sharing Cyber Threat Indicators and Defensive Measures Under the Act
Sections 104(c)	Section 106(b)(1)	• Sharing for a cybersecurity purpose. Section 104(c) • Sharing cyber threat indicators & defensive measures. Section 104(c) and 106(b)(1) • Removal prior to sharing using a manual or technical means of information not directly related to a cybersecurity threat that the private entity knows at the time of sharing to be personal information of a specific person or information identifying a specific person. Section 104(d)(2)(A) and (B) • Implement and utilize a security control to protect against unauthorized access to or acquisition of cyber threat indicators or defensive measures. Section 104(d)(1) • When receiving cyber threat indicators observe lawful restrictions placed by a private entity. Section 104(c)(2)	• Liability protection for sharing and receiving cyber threat indicators. Section 106 • Antitrust Exemption. Section 104(e) Imposition of lawful restrictions on private entity on sharing and use of cyber threat indicators or defensive measures. Section 104(c)(2)